Hope
in
Times *of* Grief

compiled by
JoNancy Sundberg

WaterBrook

Hope in Times of Grief
Published by WaterBrook Press
12265 Oracle Boulevard, Suite 200
Colorado Springs, Colorado 80921

All Scripture quotations, unless otherwise indicated, are taken from the *Holy Bible, New International Version*®. NIV®. Copyright © 1973, 1978, 1984 by International Bible Society. Used by permission of Zondervan Publishing House. All rights reserved. Scripture quotations marked (KJV) are taken from the King James Version.

ISBN 978-0-87788-394-4

Published in the United States by WaterBrook Multnomah, an imprint of the Crown Publishing Group, a division of Random House Inc., New York.

WATERBROOK and its deer colophon are registered trademarks of Random House Inc.

Library of Congress Cataloging-in-Publication Data
Sundberg, JoNancy.
    Hope in times of grief / compiled by JoNancy Sundberg.
       p. cm.
    1. Consolation—Quotations. maxims, etc. 2. Bible—Quotations.
I. Sundberg, JoNancy, 1939–
    BV4905.2.H594 1998
    242'.4—dc21
                                                97-52292

Printed in the United States of America
2009

10 9 8 7 6 5 4

SPECIAL SALES
Most WaterBrook Multnomah books are available at special quantity discounts when purchased in bulk by corporations, organizations, and special-interest groups. Custom imprinting or excerpting can also be done to fit special needs. For information, please e-mail SpecialMarkets@WaterBrookMultnomah.com or call 1-800-603-7051.

CONTENTS

Introduction   5

1 The Initial Shock . . . His Peace   9

2 Our Tears . . . His Comfort   13

3 Our Fear . . . His Care   21

4 Our Despair . . . His Hope   27

5 Our Uncertainty and
   Confusion . . . His Guidance   35

6 Our Weakness . . . His Strength   43

7 Our Distress . . . His Promises   49

8 Our Loneliness . . . His Presence   61

9 Our Acceptance . . . His Joy   73

10 A New Kind of Normalcy . . .
   His Blessing   85

Acknowledgments   96

ABBREVIATIONS

The Scripture versions quoted in this book use the following abbreviations:

AMP	Amplified New Testament
KJV	King James Version
THE MESSAGE	
NASB	New American Standard Bible
NCV	New Century Version
NEB	New English Bible
NIV	New International Version
NKJV	New King James Version
NLT	New Living Translation
NRSV	New Revised Standard Version
PHILLIPS	Phillips' Translation
RSV	Revised Standard Version
TLB	The Living Bible

See acknowledgments on page 96.

INTRODUCTION

Affliction is a universal problem. Rich, poor, educated, uneducated, cultured, barbaric, city dwellers, farmers, bank presidents, street sweepers, musicians, coal miners, old, young, Eastern, Western—all people of every tribe, nation and language group have experienced and are experiencing and will experience some form of suffering, troubles, disappointments, or tragedy, and will continue to do so in their daily lives.

—*Edith Schaeffer*, **Affliction**

For the Lord does not abandon anyone forever. Though he brings grief, he also shows
compassion according to the greatness of
his unfailing love. For he does not enjoy
hurting people or causing them sorrow.
—*Lamentations 3:31-33, NLT*

Grief is the heart's response to any deep
loss. . . . the word grief is all-inclusive. There
are many deaths in life, and we grieve for all
of them. We mourn prolonged loss of em-
ployment, death of a pet, infertility, death of
our dreams, divorce, moving, losses caused
by aging and disease. We grieve all endings
on the way to new beginnings. And all the
griefs change us.
—*Paula D'Arcy,* When Your Friend Is Grieving

May our Lord Jesus Christ himself and God
our Father (who has loved us and given us
unending encouragement and unfailing
hope by his grace) inspire you with courage
and confidence in every good thing you say
or do.
—*2 Thessalonians 2:16-17, PHILLIPS*

The most determinative thing about the way
we live our lives and most certainly the way
we walk through the valleys is what we, in

the deepest part of our beings, believe God
is like.

—*Verdell Davis,* Riches Stored in Secret Places

Job cried out to God to answer his ques-
tions. . . . Ultimately the only answer God
gave to Job was a revelation of Himself.
"Job, I am your answer." Job was not asked
to trust a plan but a Person, a personal God
who is sovereign, wise, and good. It was as
if God said to Job, "Learn who I am. When
you know me, you know enough to handle
anything."

—*R. C. Sproul,* Surprised by Suffering

God is still God. God always has been and
always will be. And, though all we may be
able to do right now is cling to Who God is
and What God is, that's enough. We may not
be able to praise. We may not be able to sing.
We may not even be able to pray, but we can
hang on to the conviction that God is God.
With David we can look ahead and say, "I
will yet praise God."

—*Roger Palm,* Bible Readings on Hope

All your waves and billows have gone over
me, and floods of sorrow pour upon me like
a thundering cataract. Yet day by day the

Lord also pours out his steadfast love upon me, and through the night I sing his songs and pray to God who gives me life. "O God my Rock," I cry, "why have you forsaken me?" . . . But O my soul, don't be discouraged. Don't be upset. Expect God to act! For I know that I shall again have plenty of reason to praise him for all that he will do. He is my help! He is my God!

—*Psalm 42:7-9, 11, TLB*

I thought I could describe a state; make a map of sorrow. Sorrow, however, turns out to be not a state but a process. . . . There is something new to be chronicled every day. Grief is like a long valley, a winding valley where any bend may reveal a totally new landscape. . . . Not every bend does. Sometimes the surprise is the opposite one; you are presented with exactly the same sort of country you thought you had left behind miles ago.

—*C. S. Lewis,* A Grief Observed

Frail children of dust, and feeble as frail,
In Thee do we trust, nor find Thee to fail:
Thy mercies how tender, how firm to the
     end,
Our Maker, Defender, Redeemer, and
     Friend.

—*Robert Grant, "O Worship the King"*

The Initial Shock . . .
His Peace

When we have experienced the shock of a major loss, sometimes our minds go into neutral. . . . The mind is paralyzed and overloaded.

—**Raymond R. Mitsch and Lynn Brookside,**
Grieving the Loss of Someone You Love

I have told you all this so that you may have peace in me. Here on earth you will have many trials and sorrows. But take heart, because I have overcome the world.

—**John 16:33,** *NLT*

I felt like I was having a nightmare. I wanted to wake up. I prayed to wake up. A strong sense of disbelief, of unreality, swept over me.

—*Mary White,* Harsh Grief, Gentle Hope

If only my anguish could be weighed
   and all my misery be placed on the
      scales!
It would surely outweigh the sand of the
      seas.

—*Job 6:2-3, NIV*

Come, ye disconsolate, wherever ye
      languish—
Come to the mercy-seat, fervently kneel;
Here bring your wounded hearts,
Here tell your anguish;
Earth has no sorrow that heaven cannot heal.

—*Sir Thomas Moore, "Come Ye Disconsolate"*

The mountains may disappear,
   and the hills may come to an end,
but my love will never disappear;
   my promise of peace will not come to
      an end.

—*Isaiah 54:10, NCV*

Let not your heart be troubled. . . . Let the peace of God rule in your hearts.

—*John 14:1; Colossians 3:15, KJV*

If we open the shutters in the morning, the light will pour in. We do not need to beseech it to pour in. It will pour in if we will let it. It is so with the peace of God. It will rule in our hearts if only we will let it in.
—*Amy Carmichael,* Edges of His Ways

The gentle past, the horror-filled future— neither is a good place for the mind to dwell. Knowing that God is in control today is the underlying peace that passes understanding.
—*Jeri Krumroy,* Grief Is Not Forever

You will keep in perfect peace all who
    trust in you,
  whose thoughts are fixed on you!
—*Isaiah 26:3,* NLT

Our Lord did not say, These things I have spoken unto you, that in your circumstances ye might have peace; or, these things I have spoken unto you that in the love of others ye might have peace; but He did say, "These things"—things of wonder, joy, sorrow, preparation—"I have spoken unto you, that in Me ye might have peace." (John 15:20) Is there any surprise of grief that our dear Lord has not foreseen? "These things I have spoken unto you, that *in Me ye might have peace.*"
—*Amy Carmichael,* Edges of His Ways

When peace like a river attendeth my way,
When sorrows like sea billows roll;
Whatever my lot,
Thou has taught me to say,
"It is well, it is well with my soul."
—*Horatio G. Spafford, "It Is Well with My Soul"*

Now may the Lord of peace himself give
you peace at all times and in every way. The
Lord be with all of you.
—*2 Thessalonians 3:16, NIV*

Our Tears . . . His Comfort

But why celebrate stoic tearlessness? Why insist on never outwarding the inward when that inward is bleeding? Does enduring while crying not require as much strength as never crying? Must we always mask our suffering? May we not sometimes allow people to see and enter it? . . . I shall look at the world through tears. Perhaps I shall see things that dry-eyed I could not see.

—**Nicholas Wolterstorff,** *Lament for a Son*

Then I saw a new heaven and a new earth, for the first heaven and the first earth had passed away. . . . And I heard a loud voice from the throne saying, "Now the dwelling of God is with men, and he will live with them. They will be his people, and God himself will be with them and be their God. He will wipe every tear from their eyes. There will be no more death or mourning or crying or pain, for the old order of things has passed away."

—**Revelation 21:1, 3-4,** *NIV*

Suffering is a universal language. Tears are the same for Jews or Muslims or Christians, for white or black or brown, for children or adults or the elderly. When life hurts and our dreams fade, we may express our anguish in different ways, but each one of us knows the sting of pain and heartache, disease and disaster, trials and sufferings.

—*Charles R. Swindoll,* Hope Again

There is a sacredness in tears. They are not the mark of weakness, but of power. They speak more eloquently than ten thousand tongues. They are messengers of overwhelming grief, of deep contrition, and of unspeakable love.

—*Washington Irving*

When we are faced with deep loss, we are catapulted into a crucible of grief, drenched with tears. God has equipped us with the ability to weep to help us process our losses.

—*Jan Frank,* A Graceful Waiting

I weep with grief; my heart is heavy with sorrow; encourage and cheer me with your words.

—*Psalm 119:28,* TLB

I have heard your prayer. I have seen your tears; surely I will heal you.
—*2 Kings 20:5, NKJV*

Weeping is NOT something which Christians are not supposed to do or to feel. Hot tears sliding down our cheeks, salty in the corner of our lips, is not a wrong thing to feel as part of our experience of life. It is only when the final enemy is destroyed and the last victory is won that all tears are to be wiped away. Until then we are meant to weep with those who weep, as well as to rejoice with those who rejoice. . . . It is God who will wipe away all tears.
—*Edith Schaeffer,* Affliction

Thank God, bless God, all who suffer not
More grief than he can weep for; . . . for
        tears will run
Soon in long rivers down the lifted face,
And leave the vision clear for stars and
        sun.
—*Elizabeth Barrett Browning*

Blessed are those whose strength is in you [Lord], who have set their hearts on pilgrimage. As they pass through the Valley of Baca [tears], they make it a place of springs; the autumn rains also cover it with pools. They go from strength to strength, till each appears before God in Zion.

—*Psalm 84:5-7, NIV, adapted*

To weep is to make less the depth of grief.
—*William Shakespeare*

Jesus, what a Help in sorrow!
While the billows o'er me roll,
Even when my heart is breaking,
He, my Comfort, helps my soul.
—*J. Wilbur Chapman, "Our Great Savior"*

He heals the brokenhearted and binds up their wounds (curing their pains and their sorrows).
—*Psalm 147:3, AMP*

The tears . . . streamed down, and I let them flow as freely as they would, making them a pillow for my heart. On them it rested.
—*St. Augustine, Confessions*

As one whom his mother comforts, so I will comfort you.
—*Isaiah 66:13, NASB*

(God) not only knows your tears, but He records them and retains them! Why? So that one day He may transform them into gems of joy and glory. No tears are ever wasted when you follow Him.

—*Warren Wiersbe,* With the Word

Take the name of Jesus with you,
Child of sorrow and of woe;
It will joy and comfort give you—
Take it, then, where'er you go.

—*Lydia Baxter, "Take the Name of Jesus with You"*

Surely He has borne our griefs and carried our sorrows.

—*Isaiah 53:4, NKJV*

For he has not despised or disdained
    the suffering of the afflicted one;
he has not hidden his face from him
    but has listened to his cry for help.

—*Psalm 22:24, NIV*

How oft in the conflict,
when pressed by the foe,
I have fled to my Refuge
and breathed out my woe;
How often, when trials
like sea billows roll,
Have I hidden in Thee,
O thou Rock of my soul.

—*William O. Cushing, "Hiding in Thee"*

Grief and sorrow become a divine rendez-vous with the Prince of Peace, the Father of mercies, and the Spirit who "intercedes for us with groanings too deep for words" (Romans 8:26, NASB). Paradoxically, our most treasured times become not the mountaintop experiences, but the valleys of despair . . . . We cannot truly weep for joy until we have wept for sorrow.

—*Jan Frank,* A Graceful Waiting

In the multitude of my anxious thoughts within me, your comforts cheer and delight my soul!

—*Psalm 94:19, AMP*

No matter how deep our darkness, He is deeper still.

—*Corrie ten Boom*

I, even I, am He who comforts you. . . . I have covered you with the shadow of My hand.

—*Isaiah 51:12,16, NKJV*

He hideth my soul in the cleft of the rock
That shadows a dry, thirsty land;
He hideth my soul in the depths of His
    love,
And covers me there with His hand.

—*Fanny J. Crosby, "He Hideth My Soul"*

Love is why He came. . . . Every tear we shed becomes His tear. He may not yet wipe them away, but He makes them His. Would we rather have our own dry eyes, or His tear-filled ones? He came. He is here. That is the salient fact.

—*Peter Kreeft,* Making Sense Out of Suffering

Notice that the basis of Jesus' comfort is not well-wishing of the sort we give. His comfort is substantial because it is grounded in the love of God. This is a needed reminder that the only source of true comfort is in Christ Himself. We cannot have peace, security, and hope without Christ. Christ is the only source of comfort and the only way to the Father.

—*Tabletalk Magazine,* Ligonier Ministries

We know the love that God has for us, and we trust that love. God is love.

—*1 John 4:16, NCV*

For I am convinced that nothing can ever separate us from his love. Death can't, and life can't. The angels won't, and all the powers of hell itself cannot keep God's love away. Our fears for today, our worries about tomorrow, or where we are—high above the sky, or in the deepest ocean—nothing will ever be able to separate us from the love of God demonstrated by our Lord Jesus Christ when he died for us.

—*Romans 8:38-39,* TLB

When we are perplexed and troubled by our suffering, we err if we charge Him with being indifferent to our pain and anguish, or spiteful and vindictive. God is love, and because we are the objects and recipients of His love, we may safely trust ourselves to His providence—silent and mysterious though it seems to be.

—*Herbert Lockyer,* Dark Threads the Weaver Needs

All praise to the God and Father of our Lord Jesus Christ. He is the source of every mercy and the God who comforts us. He comforts us in all our troubles so that we can comfort others. When others are troubled, we will be able to give them the same comfort God has given us.

—*2 Corinthians 1:3-4,* NLT

Our Fear . . . His Care

But now, thus says the Lord, who created you . . . "Fear not, for I have redeemed you; I have called you by your name; you are Mine. When you pass through the waters, I will be with you; And through the rivers, they shall not overflow you. When you walk through the fire, you shall not be burned, Nor shall the flame scorch you. For I am the LORD your God, the Holy One of Israel, your Savior."

—Isaiah 43:1-3, *NKJV*

So do not fear, for I am with you; do not be dismayed, for I am your God. I will strengthen you and help you; I will uphold you with my righteous right hand.

—Isaiah 41:10, *NIV*

Don't be afraid. Just stand where you are and watch, and you will see the wonderful way the Lord will rescue you today.
—*Exodus 14:13, TLB*

Do not be afraid; do not be discouraged. Go out to face them tomorrow, and the Lord will be with you.
—*2 Chronicles 20:17, NIV*

Do not fear tomorrow. God is already there. ✓
—*Anonymous*

Give your entire attention to what God is doing right now, and don't get worked up about what may or may not happen tomorrow. God will help you deal with whatever hard things come up when the time comes.
—*Matthew 6:34, THE MESSAGE*

For God has not given us a spirit of fear, but of power and of love and of a sound mind.
—*2 Timothy 1:7, NKJV*

I sought the Lord, and He heard me, and delivered me from all my fears.
—*Psalm 34:4, NKJV*

Peace I leave with you; my peace I give you. I do not give to you as the world gives. Do not let your hearts be troubled and do not be afraid.

—*John 14:27, NIV*

Don't worry about anything; instead, pray about everything; tell God your needs and don't forget to thank him for his answers. If you do this you will experience God's peace, which is far more wonderful than the human mind can understand. His peace will keep your thoughts and your hearts quiet and at rest as you trust in Christ Jesus.

—*Philippians 4:6-7, TLB*

Sorrow looks back.
Worry looks around.
Faith looks up.

—*Anonymous*

Hidden in the hollow of His blessed hand,
Never foe can follow, never traitor stand;
Not a surge of worry, not a shade of care,
Not a blast of hurry touch the spirit there.

—*Frances R. Havergal, "Like a River Glorious"*

Give your worries to the Lord,
 and he will take care of you.
 He will never let good people down.

—*Psalm 55:22, NCV*

God is our refuge and strength, always ready to help in times of trouble. So we will not fear.

—*Psalm 46:1-2, NLT*

Yes, because God's your refuge, the High
  God your very own home,
Evil can't get close to you, harm can't get
  through your door.
He ordered his angels to guard you
  wherever you go.
If you stumble, they'll catch you; their job
  is to keep you from falling.

—*Psalm 91:9-12, THE MESSAGE*

The eternal God is your refuge, and underneath are the everlasting arms.

—*Deuteronomy 33:27, NKJV*

What have I to dread, what have I to fear,
Leaning on the everlasting arms?
I have blessed peace with my Lord so near,
Leaning on the everlasting arms.

—*Elisha A. Hoffman, "Leaning on the Everlasting Arms"*

God is big enough and wise enough to handle our cares.

—*Anonymous*

If God is what He would seem to be from His revealings; if He is indeed the "God of all comfort" (2 Corinthians 1:3); if He is our Shepherd; if He is really and truly our Father; if, in short, all the many aspects He has told us of His character and His ways are actually true, then we must come to the positive conviction that He is, in Himself alone, enough for all our needs and that we may safely rest in Him absolutely and forever.
—*Hannah Whitall Smith,* God of All Comfort

Thy bountiful care what tongue can recite?
It breathes in the air, it shines in the light;
It streams from the hills, it descends to the
     plain,
And sweetly distills in the dew and the
     rain.
—*Robert Grant, "O Worship the King"*

"Because he loves me," says the
    Lord, "I will rescue him;
I will protect him, for he
    acknowledges my name.
He will call upon me, and I will
    answer him;
I will be with him in trouble,
I will deliver him and honor him."
—*Psalm 91:14-15, NIV*

I cried out to the Lord in my
   suffering, and he heard me.
He set me free from all my fears.
—*Psalm 34:6, NLT*

Does Jesus care when my way is dark
With a nameless dread and fear?
As the daylight fades into deep night
   shades,
Does He care enough to be near?
O yes, He cares—I know He cares!
His heart is touched with my grief;
When the days are weary, the long nights
   dreary,
I know my Saviour cares.
—*Frank E. Graeff, "Does Jesus Care?"*

Whoever trusts in the Lord is kept safe.
—*Proverbs 29:25, NIV*

You are exalted high above every star and
galaxy in the entire cosmos . . . yet You are
also "the God of all mankind," the great,
personally present, personally involved God
who loves, rescues, and takes care of all who
trust You.
—*Ruth Myers,* 31 Days of Praise

Our Despair . . . His Hope

This is the stage of a solemn inertia. And here is a new level of pain. . . . This pain is called despair. . . . The quality that characterizes grieving now is hopelessness. . . . The griever expects nothing to follow. The worst moment of grief, then, is hopelessness. To be altogether without hope is to despair.

— **Walter Wangerin, Jr.,** *Mourning into Dancing*

For now we see through a mirror, dimly; but then face to face. Now I know in part, but then shall I know just as I also am known.

—**1 Corinthians 13:12,** *NKJV*

Why am I so sad?
    Why am I so upset?
I should put my hope in God
    and keep praising him,
    my Savior and my God.

—**Psalm 43:5,** *NCV*

No one ever told me that grief felt so like fear. I am not afraid, but the sensation is like being afraid. The same fluttering in the stomach, the same restlessness, the yawning. I keep on swallowing.

—*C. S. Lewis,* A Grief Observed

There's more to come: We continue to shout our praise even when we're hemmed in with troubles, because we know how troubles can develop passionate patience in us, and how that patience in turn forges the tempered steel of virtue, keeping us alert for whatever God will do next. In alert expectancy such as this, we're never left feeling short-changed. Quite the contrary—we can't round up enough containers to hold everything God generously pours into our lives through the Holy Spirit!

—*Romans 5:3-5,* THE MESSAGE

No one moves from despair to emotional recovery in a straight line—no matter what level of grief we're dealing with. Grief comes in waves. Just about the time we take a deep breath and say, "OK, I can get through this," we get hit again.

—*Sandra Aldrich,* Living Through the Loss of Someone You Love

I am he who will sustain you.
I have made you and I will carry you;
I will sustain you and I will rescue you.

—*Isaiah 46:4, NIV*

I would have lost heart, unless I had believed that I would see the goodness of the Lord in the land of the living.

—*Psalm 27:13, NKJV*

True hope changes sorrow, but does not obliterate it.

—*Edith Schaeffer, Affliction*

We have this hope as an anchor for the soul, firm and secure.

—*Hebrews 6:19, NIV*

Hope is like an anchor. Our hope in Christ stabilizes us in the storms of life, but unlike an anchor, it does not hold us back.

—*Anonymous*

God does not condemn our moments of despair and unbelief. He Himself set the tone by diving into the earth and enduring cruel, senseless suffering. Before the final moment, His own Son asked if the cup could pass from Him, and on the cross cried out,

"God, why have You forsaken me?" The full range of anger and despair and blackness . . . is present in the Christian message—complete identification with the suffering world.

—*Philip Yancey*, Where Is God When It Hurts?

When through fiery trials thy pathway
    shall lie,
My grace, all sufficient, shall be thy
    supply:
The flame shall not hurt thee; I only design
Thy dross to consume and thy gold to
    refine.

—*"How Firm a Foundation"*

Friends, when life gets really difficult, don't jump to the conclusion that God isn't on the job. Instead, be glad that you are in the very thick of what Christ experienced. This is a spiritual refining process, with glory just around the corner.

—*1 Peter 4:12-13*, THE MESSAGE

But He knows the way that I take (He has concern for it, appreciates, and pays attention to it). When He has tried me, I shall come forth as refined gold (pure and luminous).

—*Job 23:10*, AMP

I praise You for Your sovereignty over the broad events of my life and over the details. With You, nothing is accidental, nothing is incidental, and no experience is wasted. And every trial that You allow to happen is a platform on which You reveal Yourself, showing Your love and power, both to me and to others looking on.

—*Ruth Myers,* 31 Days of Praise

Hope does not lie solely in anticipating that God will give us a wonderful future and resolve all things to our good. Rather, hope lies in knowing that God is with us in the here and now, and He will impart His love and grace to us to enable us to go from minute to minute, hour to hour, day to day.

—*Charles Stanley,* The Reason for My Hope

Let Thy unfailing love, O Lord, rest upon us, as we have put our hope in Thee. . . .
This one thing I know: God is for me!
—*Psalm 33:22, NEB; Psalm 56:9, TLB*

Suffering teaches us the absolute limits to our abilities.
—*Anonymous*

We are hard pressed on every side, yet not crushed; we are perplexed, but not in despair; persecuted, but not forsaken; struck down, but not destroyed—always carrying about in the body the dying of the Lord Jesus, that the life of Jesus also may be manifested in our body.

—*2 Corinthians 4:8-10, NKJV*

Our Lord Jesus Christ himself . . . which hath loved us, and hath given us everlasting consolation and good hope through grace, comfort your hearts.

—*2 Thessalonians 2:16-17, KJV*

Grace teaches us in the midst of life's greatest comforts to be willing to die and in the midst of its greatest crises to be willing to live.

—*Anonymous*

Why does God bring thunderclouds and disasters when we want green pastures and still waters? Bit by bit we find, behind the clouds, the Father's feet; behind the thunder, "a still small voice" that comforts with a comfort that is unspeakable.

—*Oswald Chambers,* In the Presence of His Majesty

Your sun will set no more,
Neither will your moon wane;

For you will have the Lord for an
    everlasting light,
And the days of your mourning will be
    finished.
—*Isaiah 60:20,* NASB

I have found that the human spirit can withstand almost any tragedy, if we can make sense of it or at least believe that God is in control. We . . . know that no interruption [in life], be it tragic or delightful, is greater than our God. He can bring hope into inexplicable loss.
—*M. Craig Barnes,* When God Interrupts

God says that the more hopeless your circumstances, the more likely your salvation. The greater your cares, the more genuine your prayers. The darker the room, the greater the need for light. . . . God's help is near and always available, but it is only given to those who seek it.
—*Max Lucado,* He Still Moves Stones

You may have to go through deep waters, but the good news is that you will go through them. . . . The outcome is certain. God will win, and because He wins and you are in Him, you will win too.
—*Charles Stanley,* The Reason for My Hope

In all things it is better to hope than to despair.

—*Goethe*

You will surely forget your trouble,
  recalling it only as waters gone by.
Life will be brighter than noonday,
  and darkness will become like morning.
You will be secure, because there is hope;
  you will look about you and take your
    rest in safety.

—*Job 11:16-18, NIV*

Other men see only a hopeless end, but the Christian rejoices in an endless hope.

—*Gilbert Beenken*

Those who hope in me will not be disappointed.

—*Isaiah 49:23, NIV*

Our Uncertainty and Confusion . . . His Guidance

This is what the Lord says—
 your Redeemer, the Holy One of Israel:
"I am the Lord your God,
 who teaches you what is best for you,
 who directs you in the way you should
  go."
—Isaiah 48:17, *NIV*

Pain. We all know what it tastes like. Whether its source is physical, emotional, mental, or spiritual, its interruption in our lives disrupts and reshapes. It intercepts our hopes and plans; it rearranges our dreams. It always leaves a mark.

—Tim Hansel, ***You Gotta Keep Dancin'***

Trust in the Lord with all your heart,
 and do not rely on your own insight.
In all your ways acknowledge him,
 and he will make straight your paths.
—Proverbs 3:5-6, *RSV*

We've been surrounded and battered by troubles, but we're not demoralized; we're not sure what to do, but we know that God knows what to do.

—2 Corinthians 4:8, THE MESSAGE

Guide me, O Thou great Jehovah,
Pilgrim through this barren land;
I am weak, but Thou art mighty;
Hold me with Thy pow'rful hand.

—William Williams, "Guide Me, O Thou Great Jehovah"

If it were possible for me to alter any part of His plan, I could only spoil it.

—John Newton, The Works of John Newton

You do not know what a day may bring forth.

—Proverbs 27:1, NKJV

Not for one single day
Can I discern my way,
  But this I surely know,
Who gives the day,
Will show the way
  So I securely go.

—John Oxenham, Bees in Amber

You chart the path ahead of me.

—Psalm 139:3, NLT

My life is but a weaving betwixt my God
  and me:
I do not choose the colors He worketh
  steadily.
Sometimes He weaveth sorrow, and I in
  foolish pride
Forget He sees the upper and I the
  underside.
Not till the loom is silent and the shuttles
  cease to fly
Will God unfold the pattern and explain
  the reason why.
For the dark threads are as needful in the
  Weaver's skillful hand
As the threads of gold and silver in the
  pattern He has planned.
—*Grant Tuller*

"For I know the plans I have for you," de-
clares the Lord, "plans to prosper you and
not to harm you, plans to give you hope and
a future."
—*Jeremiah 29:11, NIV*

God has a thousand ways
Where I can see not one;
When all my means have reached their
  end,
Then His have just begun.
—*Esther Guyot*

Lord, we often come to you with muddled ideas, unsure of what is best. Thank you, Father, for the assurance that our imperfect prayers cannot hinder your incredible power.

—*Max Lucado,* God's Inspirational Promise Book

As for God, his way is perfect.
—*Psalm 18:30, KJV*

Tell me what to do, O Lord, and make it plain.
—*Psalm 27:11, TLB*

All the way my Savior leads me;
What have I to ask beside?
Can I doubt His tender mercy,
Who through life has been my Guide?
—*Fanny J. Crosby, "All the Way My Savior Leads Me"*

Come to Me, all you who labor and are heavy laden and I will give you rest. Take My yoke upon you and learn from Me, for I am gentle and lowly in heart, and you will find rest for your souls. For My yoke is easy and My burden is light.
—*Matthew 11:28-30, NKJV*

When life's dark maze I tread
And griefs around me spread,
Be Thou my guide;
Bid darkness turn to day,
Wipe sorrow's tears away,
Nor let me ever stray from Thee aside.

—*Ray Palmer. "My Faith Looks Up to Thee"*

The Lord will guide you always;
   he will satisfy your needs.

—*Isaiah 58:11, NIV*

I am trusting Thee to guide me—
Thou alone shalt lead,
Ev'ry day and hour supplying
All I need.
I am trusting Thee, Lord Jesus—
Never let me fall;
I am trusting Thee forever,
And for all.

—*Frances R. Havergal, "I Am Trusting Thee, Lord Jesus"*

Your decisions are as full of wisdom as the
oceans are with water. . . . Tell me where you
want me to go and I will go there.

—*Psalm 36:6; 86:11, TLB*

He leadeth me!
O blessed thought!
O words with heav'nly comfort fraught!
Whate'er I do,
Where'er I be,
Still 'tis God's hand that leadeth me!
—*Joseph Gilmore, "He Leadeth Me"*

You can make many plans, but the Lord's
purpose will prevail.
—*Proverbs 19:21, NLT*

Thy way, not mine, O Lord,
    However dark it be!
Lead me by thine own hand,
    Choose out the path for me.
Smooth let it be or rough,
    It will be still the best;
Winding or straight, it leads
    Right onward to thy rest.
Not mine, not mine the choice,
    In things or great or small;
Be thou my guide, my strength,
    My wisdom, and my all!
—*Horatius Bonar, "Thy Way, Not Mine"*

For this God is our God for ever and ever:
he will be our guide even unto death.
—*Psalm 48:14, KJV*

God moves in a mysterious way
His wonders to perform;
He plants His footsteps in the sea
And rides upon the storm.

You fearful saints, fresh courage take:
The clouds you so much dread
Are big with mercy, and shall break
In blessings on your head.

His purposes will ripen fast,
Unfolding every hour;
The bud may have a bitter taste,
But sweet will be the flower.

Blind unbelief is sure to err
And scan His work in vain;
God is His own interpreter,
And He will make it plain.

—*William Cowper, "God Moves in a Mysterious Way"*

Show me the path where I should go, O
Lord; point out the right road for me to
walk. . . . How I need a map—and your
commands are my chart and guide. . . .
Guide me clearly along the way you want
me to travel so that I will understand you and
walk acceptably before you.

—*Psalm 25:4; 119:19; Exodus 33:13,* TLB

Though sorrows befall us and Satan
    oppose,
God leads His dear children along;
Through grace we can conquer, defeat all
    our foes,
God leads His dear children along.
Some thro' the waters, some thro' the
    flood,
Some thro' the fire, but all thro' the blood;
Some thro' great sorrow, but God gives a
    song,
In the night season and all the day long.

—*G.A. Young, "God Leads Us Along"*

I will instruct you and teach you in the way
you should go; I will guide you with My eye.
—*Psalm 32:8, NKJV*

The Lord is good and glad to teach the
proper path to all who go astray; he will
teach the ways that are right and best to
those who humbly turn to him. And when
we obey him, every path he guides us on is
fragrant with his lovingkindness and his
truth.
—*Psalm 25:8-10, TLB*

Our Weakness . . .
His Strength

But those who wait on the Lord will find new strength. They will fly high on wings like eagles. They will run and not grow weary. They will walk and not faint.

—Isaiah 40:31, *NLT*

When . . . eaglets are old enough to learn to fly, in love the mother stirs up the nest and thrusts them out so that they will be driven to find the use of their wings. But she floats in the air under them and watches them with eyes of love, and when she sees any little eaglet showing signs of weariness, she flies beneath it and spreads out her great strong mother wings to bear it up until it is rested and ready to fly again. The Lord does the same for His children.

—Hannah Whitall Smith, *The Veil Uplitfted*

As thy days, so shall thy strength be.

—Deuteronomy 33:25, *KJV*

No one ever told me about the laziness of grief. Except at my job—where the machine seems to run on much as usual—I loathe the slightest effort. Not only writing but even reading is too much. Even shaving. What does it matter now whether my cheek is rough or smooth?

—*C. S. Lewis,* A Grief Observed

The eyes of the Lord search the whole earth in order to strengthen those whose hearts are fully committed to him.

—*2 Chronicles 16:9, NLT*

We look at ourselves—
Assess our strengths,
Cringe at our weaknesses,
Construct a box
And crawl inside.
We tell God to make a difference . . .
As long as we get to stay
inside the box.

—*Glaphre',* When the Pieces Don't Fit . . . God Makes the Difference

Give me strength, Lord, for living this hard moment to Your glory. May I honestly be willing to pay the price that is my part of the whole, because Christ died to make it possible to go on after this particular devastation.

—*Edith Schaeffer,* Affliction

For since he himself has passed through the test of suffering, he is able to help those who are meeting their test now.

—*Hebrews 2:18, NEB*

Whatever today's test may be, through accident, physical disability, our own mistakes or failures or disobedience, perhaps the hostility of others, He is able to help us meet our test.

—*Elisabeth Elliott,* A Path Through Suffering

In his kindness God called you to his eternal glory by means of Jesus Christ. After you have suffered a little while, he will restore, support, and strengthen you, and he will place you on a firm foundation. All power is his forever and ever.

—*1 Peter 5:10-11, NLT*

Whom have I in heaven but you?
    I desire you more than anything on
        earth.
My health may fail, and my spirit may
        grow weak,

but God remains the strength of my
heart;
he is mine forever.
—*Psalm 73:25-26, NLT*

My grace is sufficient for you, for My
strength is made perfect in weakness.
—*2 Corinthians 12:9, NKJV*

I cannot, but God can;
Oh, balm for all my care!
The burden that I drop
His hand will lift and bear.
Though eagle pinions tire,
I walk where once I ran,
This is my strength to know
I cannot, but He can.
—*Annie Johnson Flint*

Not that we are in any way confident of
doing anything by our own resources—our
ability comes from God.
—*2 Corinthians 3:5, Phillips*

But not of us this strength, O Lord,
And not of us this constancy.
Our trust is Thine eternal Word,
Thy presence our security.
—*Amy Carmichael*

I can do all things through Christ who strengthens me.

—*Philippians 4:13, NKJV*

Trust in the Lord forever,
For in God the Lord, we have an
    everlasting Rock.

—*Isaiah 26:4, NASB*

Sorrow is a fruit; God does not make it grow on limbs too weak to bear it.

—*Victor Hugo*

O Lord, be gracious to us;
    we long for you.
Be our strength every morning,
    our salvation in time of distress.

—*Isaiah 33:2, NIV*

When all kinds of trials and temptations crowd into your lives, my brothers, don't resent them as intruders, but welcome them as friends! Realise that they come to test your faith and to produce in you the quality of endurance.

—*James 1:2-3, Phillips*

Let us run with patient endurance and steady and active persistence the appointed course of the race that is set before us, looking away (from all that will distract) to Jesus, Who is the Leader and the Source of our faith.

—*Hebrews 12:1-2, AMP*

Father, forgive us for the times that we have questioned you; forgive us for the times we have doubted you; forgive us for the times we've shaken our heads and pounded our fists against the earth and cried, "Where are you?" For Father, we know that you have been here—you've carried us through the valley, and you've given us strength.

—*Max Lucado,* God's Inspirational Promise Book

The Sovereign Lord is my strength! He will make me as surefooted as a deer and bring me safely over the mountains.

—*Habakkuk 3:19, NLT*

The Lord is my strength and my shield; my heart trusted in him, and I am helped: therefore my heart greatly rejoiceth; and with my song will I praise him.

—*Psalm 28:7, KJV*

This day is sacred to our Lord. Do not grieve, for the joy of the Lord is your strength.

—*Nehemiah 8:10, NIV*

Our Distress . . .
His Promises

The good man does not escape all troubles—he has them too. But the Lord helps him in each and every one.

—**Psalm 34:19,** *TLB*

We experience loss whenever we lose or are deprived of something or someone we value and have become attached to. The loss may feel like a tap on the shoulder or a two by four across our forehead. The severity of the impact depends on the significance of the loss.

—**Gary Oliver,** *Real Men Have Feelings, Too*

Suffering is the common thread in all our garments.

—**Charles R. Swindoll,** *Hope Again*

My comfort in my suffering is this:
Your promise preserves my life.

—**Psalm 119:50,** *NIV*

The pain of the no more outweighs the gratitude of the once was. Will it always be so?
—*Nicholas Wolterstorff,* Lament for a Son

The Lord is righteous in all his ways
   and loving toward all he has made.
The Lord is near to all who call on him,
   to all who call on him in truth.
—*Psalm 145:17-18,* NIV

And if my heart and flesh are weak
   To bear an untried pain,
The bruised reed he will not break,
   But strengthen and sustain.
—*John Greenleaf Whittier,* The Eternal Goodness

He will be gentle. . . . He will not break the bruised reed, nor quench the dimly burning flame. He will encourage the fainthearted.
—*Isaiah 42:2-3,* TLB

Painted on canvas after canvas is the tender touch of a Creator who has a special place for the bruised and weary of the world.
—*Max Lucado,* He Still Moves Stones

The Lord is close to the brokenhearted
and saves those who are crushed in spirit.
—*Psalm 34:18,* NIV

Some things are ruined when broken, but the heart is at its best when broken.
—*Anonymous*

Father, when you were on earth you prayed. In your hours of distress, you retreated into moments of prayer. In your hours of joy, you lifted your heart and hands in prayer. Help us to be more like you in this way. Help us to make prayer a priority in our daily lives.
—*Max Lucado,* God's Inspirational Promise Book

Call to me and I will answer you and tell you great and unsearchable things you do not know.
—*Jeremiah 33:3,* NIV

I will answer them before they even call to me. While they are still talking to me about their needs, I will go ahead and answer their prayers!
—*Isaiah 65:24,* NLT

Those who mourn are lifted to safety.
—*Job 5:11,* NKJV

No matter how weak our faith may seem, when it is anchored to the unfailing promises of God's Word, we can withstand the

strongest buffeting and the most difficult suffering.
—*John E. MacArthur,* The Power of Suffering

These two things cannot change: God cannot lie when he makes a promise, and he cannot lie when he makes an oath. These things encourage us who came to God for safety. They give us strength to hold on to the hope we have been given. We have this hope as an anchor for the soul, sure and strong.
—*Hebrews 6:18-19, NCV*

In every high and stormy gale,
    My anchor holds within the veil.
On Christ, the solid Rock, I stand;
    All other ground is sinking sand.
—*Edward Mote, "The Solid Rock"*

He maketh the storm a calm, so that the waves thereof are still.
—*Psalm 107:29, KJV*

Sometimes the Lord calms the storm. Sometimes He lets the storm rage and calms His child.
—*Anonymous*

Do not lose the courage you had in the past, which has a great reward. You must hold on,

so you can do what God wants and receive what he has promised.
—*Hebrews 10:35-36, NCV*

God's promises are like the stars: the darker the night, the brighter they shine.
—*Anonymous*

I will rejoice and be glad in Thy unfailing love; for Thou hast seen my affliction and hast cared for me in my distress. Thou hast not abandoned me.
—*Psalm 31:7-8, NEB*

The Lord is faithful in all he says;
   he is gracious in all he does.
—*Psalm 145:13, NLT*

Great is Thy faithfulness, O God my Father,
There is no shadow of turning with Thee;
Thou changest not, Thy compassions,
     they fail not;
As Thou hast been, Thou forever wilt be.

Great is Thy faithfulness!
Great is Thy faithfulness!
Morning by morning new mercies I see;
All I have needed Thy hand hath provided—
Great is Thy faithfulness, Lord, unto me.
—*Thomas Chisholm, "Great Is Thy Faithfulness"*

Yet there is this one ray of hope: his compassion never ends.

—*Lamentations 3:21-22, TLB*

Standing on the promises that cannot fail
When the howling storms of doubt and
    fear assail;
By the living word of God I shall prevail—
Standing on the promises of God!

—*R. Kelso Carter, "Standing on the Promises"*

I am God, and there is no other;
I am God, and there is no one like Me . . .
Saying, "My purpose will be established,
And I will accomplish all My good
    pleasure."

—*Isaiah 46:9-10, NASB*

There is no agonizing by God, no hoping He has made the right decision, no wondering what is really best for us. God makes no mistakes.

—*Jerry Bridges,* Trusting God

He knows us far better than we know ourselves . . . and keeps us present before God. That's why we can be so sure that every detail in our lives of love for God is worked into something good.

—*Romans 8:27-28, THE MESSAGE*

The Lord will accomplish what concerns me.

—*Psalm 138:8, NASB*

Oh, give thanks to the Lord, for he is so good! For his lovingkindness is forever.

—*Psalm 118:29, TLB*

The Lord has promised good to me,
His work my hope secures;
He will my shield and portion be
As long as life endures.

—*John Newton, "Amazing Grace"*

Surely goodness and mercy shall follow me all the days of my life; and I will dwell in the house of the Lord forever.

—*Psalm 23:6, NKJV*

Yet I am confident that I will see the
　　　Lord's goodness
　　while I am here in the land of the living.
Wait patiently for the Lord.
　　Be brave and courageous.
　　Yes, wait patiently for the Lord.

—*Psalm 27:13-14, NLT*

Yet, in the maddening maze of things,
　　And tossed by storm and flood,
To one fixed trust my spirit clings:

I know that God is good!
—*John Greenleaf Whittier*

He will always give you all you need from
day to day if you will make the Kingdom of
God your primary concern.
—*Luke 12:31, TLB*

The Lord is my shepherd; I shall not want.
—*Psalm 23:l, NKJV*

Does Jesus care when my heart is pained
Too deeply for mirth and song—
As the burdens press, and the cares distress,
And the way grows weary and long?

O yes, He cares—I know He cares!
His heart is touched with my grief;
When the days are weary, the long nights
      dreary,
I know my Saviour cares.
—*Frank E. Graeff, "Does Jesus Care?"*

Your pain is mine, and mine is yours, but the
best thing is that our pain is His. Jesus bore
the cause of our pain at Calvary, and some-
day He will eliminate suffering altogether.
—*David Biebel, If God Is So Good, Why Do I
Hurt So Bad?*

In my Father's house are many mansions; if it were not so, I would have told you. I go to prepare a place for you. And if I go and prepare a place for you, I will come again and receive you to Myself; that where I am, there you may be also.

—*John 14:2-3, NKJV*

What will heaven be like? Heaven will be my eternal home with Christ. I'll just move into the part of his Father's house he prepared for me. No fixing up that home, no parts unfinished, no disappointments on moving day. No, he's prepared it, he's made it completely ready, completely perfect, completely mine.

—*Joseph Bayly,* Heaven

No one has ever seen this,
    and no one has ever heard about it.
No one has ever imagined
    what God has prepared for those
    who love him.

—*1 Corinthians 2:9, NCV*

Be still, my soul!
    the hour is hastening on
When we shall be
    forever with the Lord,

When disappointment, grief, and fear are
    gone,
Sorrow forgot, love's purest joys restored.
Be still, my soul!
    when change and tears are past,
All safe and blessed
    we shall meet at last.

—*Katharina von Schlegel, "Be Still, My Soul"*

I am the resurrection and the life. He who
believes in Me, though he may die, he shall
live. And whoever lives and believes in Me
shall never die.

—*John 11:25-26, NKJV*

Suffering makes us want to go there
[heaven]. Broken homes and broken hearts
crush our illusions that earth can keep its
promises, that it can really satisfy. Only the
hope of heaven can truly move our passions
off this world . . . and place them where they
will find their glorious fulfillment. Suffering
hurries the heart homeward.

—*Joni Eareckson Tada,* Heaven, Your Real Home

For God so loved the world that he gave his
only Son, so that everyone who believes in
him will not perish but have eternal life.

—*John 3:16, NLT*

I never saw a moor
I never saw the sea;
Yet know I how the heather looks
And what a wave must be.

I never spoke with God,
Nor visited in Heaven;
Yet certain am I of the spot
As if the chart were given.
—*Emily Dickinson*

A mighty fortress is our God,
   A bulwark never failing;
Our helper He amid the flood
   Of mortal ills prevailing.
—*Martin Luther, "A Mighty Fortress Is Our God"*

Blessed be the Lord. . . . There has not failed
one word of all His good promise.
—*1 Kings 8:56, NKJV*

Our Loneliness . . .
His Presence

To you, O Lord, I lift up my soul.
   I trust in you, my God! . . .
Turn to me and have mercy on me,
   for I am alone and in deep distress. . . .
I put my hope in you.
—Psalm 25:1-2, 16, 21, *NLT*

Father, we pray for all lonely people, especially for those who, coming home to an empty house, stand at the door hesitant, afraid to enter. May all who stand in the doorway with fear in their hearts, like the two on the Emmaus road ask the Living One in. Then, by His grace, may they find that in loneliness they are never alone, and that He peoples empty rooms with His presence.
—Edward Blaiklock, *Kathleen*

He Himself has said, "I will never desert you, nor will I ever forsake you."
—Hebrews 13:5, *NASB*

One writes that "other friends remain,"
That loss is common to the human race;
And common is the commonplace,
And vacant chaff well meant for grain.

That loss is common does not make
My own loss less bitter, rather more;
Too common! Never morning wore
To evening, but some heart did break.
—*Alfred Lord Tennyson*

How could things go on when the world has
come to an end? How could I go on in this
void? How could one person, not very big,
leave an emptiness that was galaxy-wide?
—*Sheldon Vanauken,* A Severe Mercy

Turn to me and be gracious to me,
    for I am lonely and afflicted.
The troubles of my heart have multiplied;
    free me from my anguish.
Look upon my affliction and my distress.
—*Psalm 25:16-18, NIV*

Loneliness, a natural by-product of grief, is
the result of the primary loss and all the
secondary losses. For example, if we have
lost a spouse, we also miss the nurture and
comfort of marriage, a "couple" way of life.
—*Robert Gilliam*

Death is the great leveler, so our writers have
always told us. Of course they are right. But
they have neglected to mention the
uniqueness of each death—and the soli-
tude of suffering which accompanies that
uniqueness.

—Nicholas Wolterstorff, Lament for a Son

Yet I am not alone, for my Father is with me.
—John 16:32, NIV

Thou art my Lord Who slept upon the
    pillow,
  Thou art my Lord Who calmed the
    furious sea;
What matter beating wind and tossing
    billow
  If only we are in the boat with Thee?
—Amy Carmichael, Edges of His Ways

Be strong and courageous. Do not be terri-
fied; do not be discouraged, for the Lord
your God will be with you wherever you go.
—Joshua 1:9, NIV

Christ came to earth to experience all that
we have experienced so that we would have
an advocate in heaven who has felt our pain
and our sorrow. Christ understands from
experience the realities of living in a world

contaminated by sin and death. God understands our grief. He will not abandon us in
our pain.

—*Raymond R. Mitsch and Lynn Brookside,* Grieving the Loss of Someone You Love

The loneliness and the separation from all
comfort and comforters were experienced
by Jesus, who stands in the middle of all
time and history as the most afflicted One,
the One most separated from comfort.
And—He did it so that we would never be
separated from the comfort of God as we
come to God through this One.

—*Edith Schaeffer,* Affliction

The Lord your God is with you,
   he is mighty to save.
He will take great delight in you,
he will quiet you with his love,
he will rejoice over you with singing.

—*Zephaniah 3:17, NIV*

O God, early in the morning I cry to you.
Help me to pray
And to concentrate my thoughts on you:
   I cannot do this alone.
   In me there is darkness,
But with you there is light;
   I am lonely, but you do not leave me;

I am feeble in heart, but with you there is
     help;
  I am restless, but with you there is
     peace.
—*Dietrich Bonhoeffer*

The Lord hears good people when they
     cry out to him,
  and he saves them from all their troubles.
The Lord is close to the brokenhearted,
  and he saves those whose spirits have
     been crushed.
—*Psalm 34:17-18,* NCV

I have learned when I am most alone, the
     Spirit of God accompanies me,
  when I am most afraid, the Promise of
     God comforts me,
  when I am most fragile, the Hand of
     God upholds me.
—*James E. Miller,* Winter Grief, Summer Grace

Never a trial that He is not there,
Never a burden that He doth not bear,
Never a sorrow that He doth not share,
Moment by moment, I'm under His care.
—*Daniel W. Whittle, "Moment by Moment"*

David's confidence [in Psalm 23] was
rooted in the absolute certainty of the pres-

ence of God. He understood that with a Divine vocation comes Divine assistance and the absolute promise of Divine presence. God will not send us where He refuses to go Himself.

—*R.C. Sproul,* Surprised by Suffering

As the mountains surround Jerusalem,
   so the Lord surrounds his people
   both now and forevermore.

—*Psalm 125:2, NIV*

Give us grace to match our trials. Give us a sense of hope and purpose beyond our pain. And give us fresh assurance that we're not alone, that Your plan has not been aborted though our suffering intensifies.

—*Charles R. Swindoll,* Hope Again

Can you *trust* God, i.e. is He dependable in times of adversity? . . . Can *you* trust God? Do you have such a relationship with God and such a confidence in Him that you believe He is with you in your adversity even though you do not see any evidence of His presence and His power? . . . In order to trust God we must know Him in an intimate, personal way.

—*Jerry Bridges,* Trusting God

And those who know Your name will put their trust in You; for You, Lord, have not forsaken those who seek You.

—*Psalm 9:10, NKJV*

Grief is the same, despite the differences in its intensities; grief is always our pulley back to God.

—*Walter Wangerin, Jr.*, Mourning into Dancing

As the deer pants for the water brooks, so pants my soul for You, O God. My soul thirsts for God, for the living God.

—*Psalm 42:1-2, NKJV*

How suddenly comforting it was
   to lose the false comforts of the past!
I had long feared losing them,
   and now it was a joy to throw them
      away.
Truly it was you who put them far from
      me,
   my true and supreme comfort;
You put them far away
   and set yourself in their place.

—*St. Augustine*, Confessions

Be still, and know that I am God.

—*Psalm 46:10, NKJV*

What matters most is not knowing what we are, what we do, or what we feel; it is becoming acquainted with God, getting to know what He is and what He feels. Comfort and peace can never come from anything we know about ourselves but only and always from what we know about God.

—*Hannah Whitall Smith,* God of All Comfort

God . . . is the blessed controller of all things, the king over all kings and the master of all masters.

—*1 Timothy 6:15,* PHILLIPS

Since my youth, O God, you have taught me,
   and to this day I declare your marvelous deeds.
Even when I am old and gray,
   do not forsake me, O God,
till I declare your power to the next generation,
   your might to all who are to come.

—*Psalm 71:17-18,* NIV

Abide with me—fast falls the eventide!
The darkness deepens—Lord, with me abide;
When other helpers fail and comforts flee,

Help of the helpless, O abide with me!
Hold Thou Thy cross before my closing
 eyes,
Shine thru the gloom and point me to the
 skies;
Heaven's morning breaks and earth's vain
 shadows flee—
In life, in death, O Lord, abide with me!
—*Henry F. Lyte, "Abide with Me"*

Jesus did not come to explain away suffer-
ing or remove it. He came to fill it with his
Presence.
—*Paul Claudel*

Whither shall I go from thy Spirit? Or
whither shall I flee from thy presence? . . .
If I take the wings of the morning, and dwell
in the uttermost parts of the sea; even there
shall thy hand lead me, and thy right hand
shall hold me.
—*Psalm 139:7, 9-10, KJV*

My help is from Jehovah who made the
mountains! And the heavens too! He will
never let me stumble, slip or fall. For he is
always watching, never sleeping. . . . He
keeps his eye upon you as you come and go,
and always guards you.
—*Psalm 121:2-4, 8, TLB*

Yea, though I walk through the valley of the shadow of death, I will fear no evil; for You are with me; Your rod and Your staff, they comfort me.

—*Psalm 23:4, NKJV*

And be sure of this—that I am with you always, even to the end of the world.

—*Matthew 28:20, TLB*

I will lie down in peace and sleep, for though I am alone, O Lord, you will keep me safe. . . . When I wake up in the morning, you are still with me!

—*Psalm 4:8, TLB; Psalm 139:18, NLT*

What God's almighty pow'r hath made
    His gracious mercy keepeth,
By morning glow or evening shade
    His watchful eye ne'er sleepeth.
The Lord is never far away,
    But, thru all grief distressing,
An ever-present help and stay,
    Our peace and joy and blessing.

—*Johann J. Schutz, "Sing Praise to God Who Reigns Above"*

I would rather walk with God in the dark than go alone in the light.

—*Mary Gardiner Brainard*

Finally, brothers, whatever is true, whatever
is noble, whatever is right, whatever is pure,
whatever is lovely, whatever is admirable—
if anything is excellent or praiseworthy—
think about such things. . . . And the God of
peace will be with you.

—*Philippians 4:8-9, NIV*

Our Acceptance . . . His Joy

I was having to bear the unbearable. If I must bear, though, I would bear it—and find the whole meaning of it, taste the whole of it. I was driven by an unswerving determination to . . . learn from sorrow whatever it had to teach.

—**Sheldon Vanauken,** *A Severe Mercy*

Dear brothers and sisters, whenever trouble comes your way, let it be an opportunity for joy. For when your faith is tested, your endurance has a chance to grow. So let it grow, for when your endurance is fully developed, you will be strong in character and ready for anything.

—**James 1:2-4,** *NLT*

Weeping may go on all night, but in the morning there is joy.

—**Psalm 30:5,** *TLB*

You can't heal a wound by saying it's not there!
—*Jeremiah 6:14, TLB*

We just keep losing things; wives, husbands, friends, health, the dreams and security of the past. Nothing stays the way it was. . . . Our experiences with . . . unwanted change are crisis moments when we must decide whether or not to leave behind the life that is gone forever. We can do that only if we believe in the ongoing creativity of God, who brings light and beauty to the dark chaos of our losses in life.
—*M. Craig Barnes,* When God Interrupts

Shall we indeed accept good from God, and shall we not accept adversity?
—*Job 2:10, NKJV*

Not till the loom is silent
  And the shuttles cease to fly
Shall God unroll the canvass
  And explain the reason why.

At last when life is over
  With Him I shall abide;
Then I shall view the pattern
  Upon the upper side.

Then I shall know the reason
    Why pain with joy entwined
Was woven in the fabric
    Of a life that God designed.

—*Anonymous*

For as the heavens are higher than the
        earth,
So are My ways higher than your ways,
And My thoughts than your thoughts.

—*Isaiah 55:9, NASB*

Letting go means that you trust in the depths
of your heart that I do love you and want to
bring blessing and good things into your
life. I am your Father who loves you, who
has your best interest at heart. I delight to
bring you good things and to bless you with
joys unspeakable. I love you both by the things
I give and the things I withhold.

—*Jan Frank,* A Graceful Waiting

One who has journeyed in a strange land
cannot return unchanged.

—*C. S. Lewis*

We know sorrow, yet our joy is inextinguish-
able.

—*2 Corinthians 6:10, PHILLIPS*

Grief is a process, not an event. ✓
—*Anonymous*

Acceptance means that I accept the process. It has been said that Jesus came not to take away suffering, but to help us make our suffering more like His and to give it meaning. Acceptance means that I allow the process to transform me into the image of God's Son. It means that I'm willing to let go of who I think I ought to be, and become who God wants me to be.
—*Tim Hansel,* You Gotta Keep Dancin'

The suffering you sent was good for me,
   for it taught me to pay attention to your
      principles.
—*Psalm 119:71, NLT*

Letting go is never easy, but we are all called to hold, with open hands, life and the things in it. . . . We become the prisoner of what we cannot let go. We become the possessor of what we give away.
—*Verdell Davis,* Riches Stored in Secret Places

I have held many things in my hands, and I have lost them all; but whatever I have placed in God's hands, that I still possess.
—*Martin Luther*

Therefore the Lord longs to be gracious to
    you,
And therefore He waits on high to have
    compassion on you.
For the Lord is a God of justice;
How blessed are all those who long for
    Him.
—*Isaiah 30:18,* NASB

God has not been trying an experiment on my
faith or love in order to find out their quality.
He knew it already. It was I who didn't.
—*C.S. Lewis,* A Grief Observed

These little troubles (which are really so
transitory) are winning for us a permanent,
glorious and solid reward out of all proportion to our pain. For we are looking all the
time not at the visible things but at the invisible. The visible things are transitory: it is the
invisible things that are really permanent.
—*2 Corinthians 4:17-18,* PHILLIPS

And Lord, I choose to look beyond my past
and present troubles in this life—this tem-
porary life—and fix my eyes on the unseen
things that will last forever. I praise You for
the eternal glory these things are piling up
for me as I choose to trust You.
—*Ruth Myers,* 31 Days of Praise

Yet what we suffer now is nothing compared
to the glory he will give us later.
—*Romans 8:18, NLT*

A few days after my husband's fatal auto-
mobile accident, I was talking with the Lord.
And I asked God, not angrily, but expec-
tantly, "Well, God, what are you going to do
with this one? How are you going to use it
for your glory?"
—*JoNancy Sundberg*

Thou bottomless fountain of all good,
    I give myself to thee out of love,
    for all I have or own is thine,
    my goods, family, church, self,
    to do with as thou wilt,
    to honour thyself by me, and by all
        mine.
—*Puritan prayer,* Valley of Vision

It doesn't matter how great the pressure is.
What really matters is where the pressure
lies, whether it comes between me and God
or whether it presses me nearer His heart.
—*Hudson Taylor*

Be glad for all God is planning for you. Be
patient in trouble, and prayerful always.
—*Romans 12:12, TLB*

I have long since quit seeking the answer to that question [why?] in my own life . . . God owes me no explanation. He has the right to do what He wants, when He wants, and how He wants. Why? Because He's God.

—*Don Baker,* Pain's Hidden Purpose

Because of the Lord's great love we are
      not consumed,
  for his compassions never fail.
They are new every morning;
  great is your faithfulness.

—*Lamentations 3:22-23, NIV*

On the other side of abandonment, all of life becomes an expression of gratitude. The journey through loss was long and filled with pain. It cost us our lives. At the bottom of the abandonment, the only thing that was left was the love of God. But to be alone with the love of God is the only way to find life again.

—*M. Craig Barnes,* When God Interrupts

Satisfy us in the morning with your
      unfailing love,
  so we may sing for joy to the end of our
      lives.
Give us gladness in proportion to our
      former misery!

—*Psalm 90:14-15, NLT*

I remember the days of long ago;
    I meditate on all your works
    and consider what your hands have
        done.
—*Psalm 143:5, NIV*

If I'm sleepless at midnight, I spend the hours in grateful reflection.
—*Psalm 63:6, THE MESSAGE*

Acceptance is saying a humble yes to God and waiting for His timing to work all things together for good (Romans 8:28).
—*Wayne Monbleau,* You Don't Find Water on the Mountaintop

Help me to see how good thy will is in all,
    and even when it crosses mine
    teach me to be pleased with it.
—*Puritan prayer,* Valley of Vision

Teach me how to live to please you, because you're my God.
—*Psalm 143:10, THE MESSAGE*

Joy is not a feeling, it is a choice. It is not based upon circumstances; it is based upon attitude. It is free, but it is not cheap. It is the by-product of a growing relationship with

Jesus Christ. It requires commitment, courage and endurance.

—*Tim Hansel,* You Gotta Keep Dancin'

Always be joyful. Keep on praying. No matter what happens, always be thankful, for this is God's will for you who belong to Christ Jesus.

—*1 Thessalonians 5:16-18, NLT*

Beloved, do not think it strange concerning the fiery trial which is to try you, as though some strange thing has happened to you, but rejoice to the extent that you partake of Christ's sufferings, that when His glory is revealed, you may also be glad with exceeding joy.

—*1 Peter 4:12-13, NKJV*

Joyful, joyful, we adore Thee,
   God of glory, Lord of love;
Hearts unfold like flowers before Thee,
   Opening to the sun above.
Melt the clouds of sin and sadness,
   Drive the dark of doubt away;
Giver of immortal gladness,
   Fill us with the light of day.

—*Henry van Dyke, "Joyful, Joyful, We Adore Thee"*

These things I have spoken to you, that My joy may be in you, and that your joy may be made full.

—*John 15:11, NASB*

God's ultimate purpose in all suffering is joy. Scripture is full of songs of praise that came out of great trials.

—*Elisabeth Elliott,* A Path Through Suffering

Sorrow and joy are not separate. Happiness and sadness may be the opposites of one another, but not joy and sorrow. In fact, it is through sorrow that one discovers a calm, abiding, indestructible joy. This is the paradox of our faith: joy is forged in sorrow.

—*Walter Wangerin, Jr.,* Mourning into Dancing

Eyes to see
Ears to hear
 'To laugh, in spirit.
JOY: It comes at a great price.
And yet it can't be bought: It is wrought.

—*Maia Kling*

You will grieve, but your grief will turn to joy.

—*John 16:20, NIV*

I will turn their mourning into gladness;
   I will give them comfort and joy instead
      of sorrow.

—*Jeremiah 31:13, NIV*

Our happiness does not depend on the work
we are doing, the place we are in, our
friends, our health, whether people notice us
or not, praise us or not, understand us or not.
No single one of the circumstances has any
power in itself to upset the joy of God.

—*Amy Carmichael,* Edges of His Ways

Not that I have already obtained all this, or
have already been made perfect, but I press
on to take hold of that for which Christ Jesus
took hold of me. Brothers, I do not consider
myself yet to have taken hold of it. But one
thing I do: Forgetting what is behind and
straining toward what is ahead, I press on
toward the goal to win the prize for which
God has called me heavenward in Christ
Jesus.

—*Philippians 3:12-14, NIV*

A New Kind of Normalcy
. . . His Blessing

Caterpillar . . . spin and die,
To live again
A butterfly.

—Christina G. Rossetti

You have delivered my life from death, my
eyes from tears, and my̆ feet from stumbling
and falling. I will walk before the Lord in
the land of the living.

—Psalm 116:8-9, *AMP*

Celebrate God all day, every day. I mean,
revel in him!

—Philippians 4:4, *THE MESSAGE*

No sermon could have accomplished this thing. Experience only: it is the personal conviction that we've come to an end that makes any new thing astounding to us. It is the deep conviction of our helplessness that makes any new life hereafter a genuine mercy of God.... We needed truly to sorrow, in order truly to rejoice.

—*Walter Wangerin, Jr.,* Mourning into Dancing

Granted, sometimes the victories are small by themselves; it's only in the comparison of how we used to be that the miracle is seen. For even the most tragic loss can be turned into good—if we'll allow it to be.

—*Sandra Aldrich,* Living Through the Loss of Someone You Love

See! The winter is past;
    the rains are over and gone.
Flowers appear on the earth;
    the season of singing has come.

—*Song of Songs 2:11-12, NIV*

Beware of looking back to what you once were when God wants you to be something you have never been.

—*Oswald Chambers*

Life can only be understood by looking back-
ward, but it must be lived by looking forward.
—*Dick Innes,* How to Mend a Broken Heart

It's not always easy to choose life, Lord
Because then we have to struggle with
    who we are
  and why we are, and who you are
And what to do with who we are,
  and why we are, and who you are.
We have to let you make us new,
  and being made anything always hurts.
Father,
Let the morning come in our hearts,
So morning can come in our lives,
  And the world that needs a word of
    hope can hear
  "Death has lost, and life has won."
—*Verdell Davis,* Riches Stored in Secret Places

Do not call to mind the former things,
Or ponder things of the past.
Behold, I will do something new,
Now it will spring forth;
Will you not be aware of it?
I will even make a roadway in the
    wilderness,
Rivers in the desert. . . .

The people whom I formed for Myself,
Will declare My praise.

—*Isaiah 43:18-19, 21, NASB*

He has given me a new song to sing, of praises to our God. Now many will hear of the glorious things he did for me, and stand in awe before the Lord, and put their trust in him.

—*Psalm 40:3, TLB*

It takes a lot of plowing to insure a good crop.... God's plow goes deep, but only that the fruit may be the more abundant, that in the end we may forget the plowing and rejoice in the blessing of bearing much fruit for Him.

—*M. R. DeHaan, M.D.,* Broken Things

Surely it was for my benefit
　　that I suffered such anguish.

—*Isaiah 38:17, NIV*

God is infinite, and when He pours Himself into us and into our abilities, we take on His capacity, not our capacity. When God pours Himself into the tasks that He calls us to do, there is no limit to how much He can multiply our efforts to accomplish His purposes.

—*Charles Stanley,* The Reason for My Hope

God is able to make all grace abound to you, so that in all things at all times, having all that you need, you will abound in every good work.

—*2 Corinthians 9:8, NIV*

Thank You that in Your gracious plan to bless and use me, You've allowed me to go through hard times, through trials that many people go through in this fallen world. How glad I am that You're so good at reaching down and making something beautiful out of even the worst situations!

—*Ruth Myers*, 31 Days of Praise

But He knows the way that I take: When He has tested me, I shall come forth as gold.

—*Job 23:10, NKJV*

Every day (with its new reasons) will I bless You (affectionately and gratefully praise You); yes, I will praise Your name for ever and ever.

—*Psalm 145:2, AMP*

So let us run the race that is before us and never give up.

—*Hebrews 12:1, NCV*

Be like the bird
That, pausing in her flight
Awhile on boughs too slight,
    Feels them give way
    Beneath her and yet sings,
Knowing that she hath wings.
—*Victor Hugo*

We are uncertain of the next step, but we are certain of God. As soon as we abandon ourselves to God and do the task He has placed closest to us, He begins to fill our lives with surprises. . . . Leave everything to Him and it will be gloriously and graciously uncertain how He will come in—but you can be certain that He will come.
—*Oswald Chambers,* My Utmost for His Highest

You are a work in progress. God is molding and fashioning you into a person with whom He wants to live forever.
—*Charles Stanley,* The Reason for My Hope

Being confident of this, that he who began a good work in you will carry it on to completion until the day of Christ Jesus.
—*Philippians 1:6, NIV*

I have come that they may have life, and that they may have it more abundantly.
—*John 10:10, NKJV*

Teach us to number our days and recognize how few they are; help us to spend them as we should.
—*Psalm 90:12, TLB*

Take my life and let it be
Consecrated, Lord, to Thee;
Take my moments and my days—
Let them flow in ceaseless praise.
Take my love—my Lord, I pour
At Thy feet its treasure store;
Take myself—and I will be
Ever, only, all for Thee.
—*Frances R. Havergal, "Take My Life, and Let It Be"*

Choose to love the Lord your God and to obey him and to cling to him, for he is your life and the length of your days.
—*Deuteronomy 30:20, TLB*

God—you're my God! I can't get enough of you! So here I am in the place of worship, eyes open, drinking in your strength and glory. In your generous love I am really living at last! My lips brim praises like fountains. I bless you every time I take a breath. My arms wave like banners of praise to you.

—*Psalm 63:1, 3-4, THE MESSAGE*

The maturing dandelion has long ago surrendered its golden petals, and has reached its crowning stage of dying. It stands ready, holding up its little life, not knowing when or where or how the wind that bloweth where it listeth may waft it away. It holds itself no longer for its own keeping, only as something shared. The delicate seed-globe must break up now; it gives and gives until it has nothing left.

—*Lilias Trotter*

But I have raised you up for this very purpose, that I might show you my power and that my name might be proclaimed in all the earth.

—*Exodus 9:16, NIV*

Therefore, my beloved brethren, be steadfast, immovable, always abounding in the work of the Lord, knowing that your labor is not in vain in the Lord.

—*1 Corinthians 15:58, NKJV*

O Master, let me walk with Thee
In lowly paths of service free;
Tell me Thy secret help me bear
The strain of toil, the fret of care.

In hope that sends a shining ray
Far down the future's broadening way,
In peace that only Thou canst give,
With Thee, O Master, let me live.

—*Washington Gladden, "O Master, Let Me Walk
with Thee"*

Let us go right into the presence of God,
with true hearts fully trusting him.

—*Hebrews 10:22, NLT*

I've thrown myself headlong into your
       arms—
   I'm celebrating your rescue.
I'm singing at the top of my lungs.
   I'm so full of answered prayers.

—*Psalm 13:5-6, THE MESSAGE*

Come, Thou Fount of ev'ry blessing,
Tune my heart to sing Thy grace;
Streams of mercy, never ceasing,
Call for songs of loudest praise.

—*Robert Robinson, "Come, Thou Fount of Every
Blessing"*

The Lord has done great things for us;
We are glad.
—*Psalm 126:3*, NASB

Giver of life, creator of all that is lovely,
    Teach me to sing the words to your
        song;
I want to feel the music of living
    And not fear the sad songs
But from them make new songs
    Composed of both laughter and tears.
—*Anonymous*

And the ransomed of the Lord shall return,
and come to Zion with singing, with everlasting joy on their heads. They shall obtain
joy and gladness, and sorrow and sighing
shall flee away.
—*Isaiah 35:10*, NKJV

Thank You that I can move into the future
non-defensively, with hands outstretched to
whatever lies ahead, for You hold the future
and You will always be with me, even to my
old age . . . and through all eternity.
—*Ruth Myers,* 31 Days of Praise

Leave the Irreparable Past in His hands, and
step out into the Irresistible Future with Him.
—*Oswald Chambers,* My Utmost for His Highest

To him who is able to keep you from falling and to present you before his glorious presence without fault and with great joy—to the only God our Savior be glory, majesty, power and authority, through Jesus Christ our Lord, before all ages, now and forevermore! Amen.

—*Jude 24-25, NIV*

ACKNOWLEDGMENTS